MW00398513

Cynthia,
Love you sis
SF

FREEDOM
THROUGH
FORGIVENESS

An Interactive Prayer Journal and Devotional

Robin Major Oliphant

Robin Major-Oliphant

ROBIN MAJOR-OLIPHANT

One2Mpower Publishing

www.one2mpower.com

Ordering Information:

Quantity sales: Special discounts are available on quantity purchases by corporations, associations, and others. For details contact the publisher at the address above.

Orders by U.S. trade bookstores and wholesalers. Please contact One2Mpower Publishing: one2mpower@gmail.com

Or visit www.one2mpower.com

Printed in the United States of America

ISBN: 9781796543254

Acknowledgments

First and foremost I would like to thank my Heavenly Father for walking with me, pouring the Holy Spirit into me and never leaving me. Father your grace, mercy and love has been more than enough and you still add more to your already perfect work.

I'm grateful for my "tribe" better known as my family; my husband and our children. Richard, you are my "equalizer", God's blessing to me, and my best friend. I thank you for your patience and for supporting, loving and standing with me during the hills and valleys of life. To our children; Destin, Diamond, Madison and Mariah, thank you for showering me with unconditional love and patience along this journey of life as I experienced the growth and healing process which allowed me to gain the knowledge and wisdom necessary to be a better mother to each of you. Although I do not have it all figured out, I am grateful to be figuring it out with the family that God has blessed me with. My love for each and every one of you is immeasurable.

Special thanks to every ministry/organization that I have had the privilege to serve within, everyone that I have served alongside, as well as everyone who has poured into me, and allow me to pour back into them. Your willingness to show me the way, allow me lead, and serve alongside me has helped me to become a better leader and steward of the gifts God has blessed me with.

Treshelle Williams, thank you for seeing the light in me, giving me your vision and allowing me to run with it. Furthermore, thank you pouring into me, as well as every leader and member of "Wife Talk" selflessly. You are a light for so many, and I am blessed to call you friend. I love you.

T'Sharin Moncrief thank you for not only supporting my vision but for all that you do with "Women of Refined Gold" to support Victims (Future Overcomers) of Domestic Violence. Your bravery and willingness to lead by sharing your story, and empower others is remarkable! You touch the hearts of so many women and children as you provide refuge, guidance and hope through Christ. I love you.

Kizmat Tention you have been a God-send. From the moment we connected I began thanking God for you. Thank you for birthing the "Broken Little Pieces" Tribe, which was timely for me, and will continue to be for many more like us. I sincerely appreciate you giving of yourself so freely, pouring into me as a mentor, and friend, as well as for allowing me to reciprocate the same to you and your "tribe". I love you boo!

Latresha Davis (Angel) thanks so much for being a mentor, writing coach, friend, sounding board and for just simply being "there". Your gifts of coaching and editing are gifts from God that I pray continue to be cultivated. You have the sweetest spirit that can calm the nerve of the most anxious author, and yet an empowering spirit that will motivate anyone to go forth boldly and "get it done"! Honorable Mention: your brand "31 Artisan Wordsmith" may you continue to be fruitful with your gifts and multiply. I love you!

To my Pastors; Pastor Travis and Jackie Greene, Thank you for taking the vision that God placed within your hearts to birth Forward City Church (FCC), and sprinting with it. You lead with love and excellence, while encouraging us all to do the same. Like for many, "The City" was exactly what I needed, when I needed it. Being a part of the FCC ministry has prompted me to go deeper in Christ through pure worship, challenged me to dream bigger and encouraged me to live and love in Christ recklessly.

Lastly, but certainly not least…

To my beloved readers, thank you for having the courage to take this journey from pieces to peace with me. My heart's prayer is that you make the intentional effort to seek peace, freedom and wholeness through the Father who will provide all that you could ever ask or think to want for.

Forgiveness is much more difficult for us as emotional-beings to even begin to think about, than it is for us to act upon. Therefore, I would like to personally and genuinely congratulate each and every one of you for making the decision to take your power back, heal and reclaim your freedom. I love and appreciate you all!

Peace and Blessings,

Robin "One2Mpower" Major-Oliphant

Table of Contents

Introduction

First of all where did this come from Holy Spirit?! This Interactive Prayer Journal and Devotional was the missing piece to "The Journey" many people have read, and often hear me speak of. If you have read my book series From Pieces to Peace, I am sure that you have wondered "How?" "How did she forgive the unforgivable sins against her?" Oftentimes, I give a casual answer something like "nothing but the grace and mercy of God"; which is very true however, it goes much deeper than that. The art of forgiveness is something that the Lord so perfectly graces us with. I don't care how many books or blogs you read, and how many inspirational videos you watch regarding the art of forgiveness, the best way…the sure way, is God's way.

SPOLIER ALERT

If you have read my book series From Pieces to Peace, you may already be aware that I myself have harbored bitterness and un-forgiveness most of my life, as well as lacked self-worth. I hid from my truths and blamed people and circumstances of the past for everything that was happening to and within me. It wasn't until I became acquainted with God, and took my healing seriously that I claimed my Freedom from my past through forgiveness.

This interactive prayer journal and devotional contains daily scriptures, prayer-prompts, and words of encouragement; from me to you that will empower you to become an active participant in reclaiming your freedom through Christ. If you're up for the challenge; ready to let God in, and willing to do the work, I invite you to stand in your truth, pray with me, and do some self-reflecting, as we journey together toward healing, deliverance, peace, and freedom, through forgiveness in Christ Jesus.

In Him we have redemption through His blood, the forgiveness of sins, in accordance with the riches of God's grace.

Ephesians 1:7 NIV

Day 1

Forgiven

By God's wonderful grace we are redeemed through Christ. However, we must first go to the Father and seek forgiveness for our transgressions so that our sins may be washed away, and our souls redeemed. He is all-seeing and all-knowing therefore, we have no reason to be ashamed of our past, find fault within ourselves, place blame or justify our sins. All that we have to do is confess our sins with courage and humility to our Father, where we will be forgiven without condition.

Prayer-Prompt

Father God,

Thank You for your grace and mercy toward me. Jesus I believe that you are Christ. I open my heart to you and grant you permission to be the Lord of my life. Forgive me Father for the sins of my past. Lead me as I boldly move forward on this new journey of peace and wholeness, through forgiveness in you.

Amen

What will you boldly ask the Father to forgive you for? Write your personal prayer of forgiveness.

Be specific, what sins of the past have you been hiding from God? He forgives you...

What truths about your past do you struggle with revealing to the Father? He still loves you...

And hope does not put us to shame, because God's love has been poured out into our hearts through the Holy Spirit, who has been given to us. You see, at just the right time, when we were still powerless, Christ died for the ungodly.

Romans 5:5-6

Day 2

Love Poured Out

Since we have been redeemed through Christ Jesus, our Father has poured His love out unto us by blessing us with His Holy Spirit, which dwells on the inside of us. Accept His love, and remain aware of His presence. When tests and trials TRY to come against you, remember that the Lord is your strength; He will provide for you, comfort and protect you. He will NEVER LEAVE YOU. Maintain a pure, prayerful heart, and remember that LOVE in the form of the Holy Spirit dwells on the inside of you!

Prayer-Prompt

Father God,

Thank you for forgiving me and releasing me from my past. Pour your love out into my heart. Help me to accept, and remain fully aware of your Holy Spirit which I welcome to dwell on the inside of me, now and forevermore. Lord help me to recognize that there is no greater love than you, and that your love will never fail me.

Amen

How will you choose to be more accepting of His love, and aware of His presence? Write a personal prayer concerning His love for you.

FREEDOM THROUGH FORGIVENESS

Write the Father a love note about how much you desire God's love.

FREEDOM THROUGH FORGIVENESS

*Forget the former things; do not dwell
on the past. See, I am doing a new
thing! Now it springs up; do you not
perceive it? I am making a way in the
wilderness and streams in the
wasteland.*

Isaiah 43:18-19 NIV

Day 3

HE's doing a New Thing

God has redeemed you, forgiven you AND your past. HE has already created your future which will be hard for you to fathom if you continue to dwell on the damages of the past. How is holding on to the past serving you, or the purpose that the Lord has for your life? Focus on Him; through His word, hold true to His promises, and He will lead you to your brand new destiny. That means that you; my friend, have to let ALL of the hurt, shame, condemnation, fear, bitterness, anxiety, worry, excuses, pain, suffering, mourning GO! YES THAT TOO! Let go so that God can do something new in your life.

Prayer-Prompt

Father God,

Thank You for my brand new life. Thank you for cleansing my soul and making me new. I open my heart and I am ready to receive all that you have in store for me. I release everything that does not serve the purpose and plans you have for my life, in order to make room for your will and your way Lord.

Amen

What (specific) relationships, mistakes and mindsets of the past will you release from your life, in exchange for what God has for you?

What specific promises of God will you choose to focus on? Incorporate the word. Write a prayer that focuses on God's promises to you.

FREEDOM THROUGH FORGIVENESS

Therefore, if anyone is in Christ, he is a new creation; old things have passed away; behold, all things have become new.

2 Corinthians 5:17 KJV

Day 4

Forgive YOU

YIKES!!! *Forgiving yourself (ourselves) requires a mental paradigm shift immediately, not tomorrow, next week, or when you feel like it but NOW! Your past is gone remember? You've let the hurt, mistakes, failures, and insecurities GO! God has made you NEW! That means you shift the way you think and speak about YOU! Forgive you! Implement positive self-talk derived from what God says about you in His word. Meditate on His words until they penetrate the depths of your heart. Don't overcomplicate it. Release yourself from that grudge you're holding against yourself NOW.*

Prayer-Prompt

Father God,

Help me to change the way that I see me. Lord, help me to stand in my truth, and teach me how to love and accept who I am, and who you have called me to be. Help me to move forward with assurance that because you have forgiven me, I have the blood bought right to forgive myself.

Amen

What grudges have you been holding against yourself? What are you forgiving yourself for?

Journal positive "I am" affirmation statements until they penetrate your heart. Example "I am worthy of love". Incorporate a personal prayer declaring His word over your life.

God saved you by his grace when you believed. And you can't take credit for this; it is a gift from God.

Ephesians 2:8 NLT

Day 5

The Gift

The most precious gift that I have ever received is God's grace. I am often overwhelmed with gratitude because of it. He is always there to guide me, pick up my broken pieces when I stumble, forgive me, and show mercy toward me when I don't get things right. You too received that same grace when you accepted Him into your life, and you have the privilege of receiving His grace day after day. It never runs out! Did you know that God expects us to extend grace to everyone just as freely as He extends it to us? As you seek the Father for grace, I challenge you to also practice extending grace to others.

Prayer-Prompt

Father God,

Thank you for the gift of grace. Thank you for giving it to me so freely and consistently Father. I ask that you help me to extend the same grace to myself and others, just as freely and as consistently as you extend it to me. I know that there is so much peace in forgiveness and I understand that the grace to forgive effortlessly is found in you.

Amen

Who will you be intentional in extending grace and mercy toward in an effort to forgive? Write a personal prayer that encompasses your desire to extend grace and mercy toward others.

There are no limits to God's grace. How will you take the limits off of your grace toward others?

FREEDOM THROUGH FORGIVENESS

But the fruit of the Spirit is love, joy, peace, longsuffering, gentleness, goodness, faith, Meekness, temperance: against such there is no law. And they that are Christ's have crucified the flesh with the affections and lusts. If we live in the Spirit, let us also walk in the Spirit. Let us not be desirous of vain glory, provoking one another, envying one another.

Galatians 5:22-26 KJV

Day 6

Pluck it Away

When we have the Holy Spirit dwelling on the inside of us, we are required to walk in the spirit, and not in the flesh. This means not reacting to the ways of the world but, responding as the Holy Spirit leads us to. After suffering from trauma; be it heartbreak, abuse or losing a loved one, oftentimes our hearts become hardened and we turn cold. It's our fleshly protection mechanism. It is important that when we build up walls, wear masks and hurt people that we repent, and ask God to pluck away the places in our hearts that are hardened, and replace them with the fruit of the Spirit.

Prayer-Prompt

Father God,

Thank you for access to you, and the fruit of the spirit. I desire to walk in spirit and in truth. Pluck my heart of all bitterness, hurt, anxiety, vanity, carnality, insecurity and sorrow. I declare that the hardened places of my heart will be superseded by joy, peace, longsuffering, gentleness, goodness, faith, meekness, and temperance.

Amen

What are the hardened places of your heart that you need God to heal? Write a personal prayer concerning the hardened places of your heart. (Be honest.)

What fruit of the spirit do you desire more of?

Bear with each other and forgive one another if any of you has a grievance against someone. Forgive as the Lord forgave you.

Colossians 3:13 NIV

Day 7

Forgive Them ALL

Overthinking, over-feeling, or trying to rationalize the idea of forgiving, really makes the process much more difficult than it has to be. Forgiveness is a **process** that we all must endure. We were forgiven by God so gracefully yet, it is something many of us struggle with far too often; and for such a long duration of time. Choose to forgive, and ask the Lord to reveal and remove any lingering hurt that is hindering you from forgiving those that you have a grievance with. Believe that He will replace the hurt with grace, mercy, and tenderheartedness. That is where you will find your healing...in forgiveness, not in holding on to the hurt.

Prayer-Prompt

Father God,

I need you help with my un-forgiveness. Help me to go to my brothers and sisters, in love and reconciliation. Soften my heart Lord, and help me to see the error of my own ways in every situation as I seek to reconcile. Father, give me the grace, mercy and tenderheartedness that I need to be more forgiving, understand, and loving toward my family and friends so that I can let go of the bitterness and hurt.

Amen.

Who specifically will you forgive today, in exchange for your freedom from bondage? Be intentional in praying for each person you seek to forgive. (Write down their names, followed by the prayer.)

Write a detailed letter of forgiveness for the people who you are holding a grudge with. (This is solely an exercise for you, not meant to be delivered.)

FREEDOM THROUGH FORGIVENESS

Get rid of all bitterness, rage and anger, brawling and slander, along with every form of malice. Be kind and compassionate to one another, forgiving each other, just as in Christ God forgave you.

Ephesians 4:31-32 NIV

Day 8

Quick

While we are going through our growing process; as "Life Happens", we will still have instances where we become offended. People may hurt us, and there will consistently be opportunity for misunderstandings. What is important is the condition of our hearts. We must be mindful to maintain a heart of forgiveness at all times. Be quick to forgive in ALL things. Don't go back to holding on to unnecessary baggage that doesn't serve you, or fulfill God's will for your life. Remember YOU ARE FREE! Let it Go, and FAST!

Prayer-Prompt

Father God,

Help me to be slow to anger or take offense as I interact with family, friends, and co-workers during life's journey. If I happen to become offended or upset, prevent me from holding on to the offense; lead me in love and with courage to the person who has offended me. Provide me with the words to speak, and purify my heart as I seek to gain wisdom, achieve peace, and find understanding in every situation quickly.

Amen

What offenses will you be intentional in forgiving quickly? (Past or present) Write a personal prayer regarding overcoming offense.

Oftentimes, when we become easily offended or upset, we are coming from a place of self-righteousness. How will you be more humble in an effort to be more forgiving?

Love is patient, love is kind. It does not envy, it does not boast, it is not proud. It does not dishonor others, it is not self-seeking, it is not easily angered, it keeps no record of wrongs. Love does not delight in evil but rejoices with the truth. It always protects, always trusts, always hopes, always perseveres.

1 Corinthians 13:4-7 NIV

Day 9

Agape

Love is tricky if we rely on our emotion, which is why it is easy for us to become bound by unforgiveness. It is important that we remember to love without conditions, and love with pure hearts and intentions. God loves us unconditionally, He does not keep a record of our wrongs, nor does He hold our past against us. Did you know that we are required to extend the same love that God gives us, to everyone? That is "Agape Love"- true love; love without conditions, condemnation or prejudice.

Prayer-Prompt

Father God,

Thank you for your pure, unconditional love that never fails me. I open my heart to give and receive love freely without prejudice or condition. I accept your love Jesus. Teach me how to love and be loved just like you love me. Continue to do a work in me that prepares me to receive all of the love that you have for me. My heart is open, and I am willing to love and be loved your way.

Amen

What boundaries or conditions will you remove in order to receive love?

What boundaries or conditions will you remove in order to give love?

Write yourself a letter about the love you desire to give to, and receive from others.

Write a personal prayer concerning unconditional love.

But seek first his kingdom and his righteousness, and all these things will be given to you as well.

Matthew 6:33 NIV

Day 10

Focus on Him

This takes practice. Again, I know...none of us are perfect but with diligence, and true intention, seeking the Father and inserting Him into every area of our lives makes it a routine of habit. Seeking the Father in all we do places Him at the center of our lives, and strengthens our walk with Him. It helps us to mature in areas of our lives where we struggle such as forgiving often, loving unconditionally, and trusting without fear.

Prayer-Prompt

Father God,

Thank you for your being my firm foundation. Teach me how to seek you in all things concerning my life, regardless of how insignificant I think they are at the time. Remind me that when I seek you there is nothing for me to figure out, because you already know the beginning and the end. Establish yourself in every areas of my life Father, and remind me to look to you for direction.

Amen

Be intentional. What area of your life will you begin to seek the Father, in exchange for peace? Write a personal prayer concerning peace.

Switch it UP. Prayer doesn't have to be drawn out or ceremonial. Take a pause and tell the Father about your day. (Write)

Now the Lord is the Spirit, and where the Spirit of the Lord is, there is freedom.

2 Corinthians 3:17 NIV

Day 11

FREE

Listen! You have come too far in the process to go back to the invisible chains of bondage now! You are FREE!!! Do not allow anyone, or anything to even attempt to hold you hostage to your past when the Lord has ALREADY granted you FREEDOM through forgiveness. Be at Peace, free from guilt, shame, and condemnation. There is nothing and no one that can hold you hostage to a past that you and the Lord have already forgiven you for! Be Free!!!

Prayer-Prompt

Father God,

Thank You for freeing me! It is in you that I live, and have been healed, delivered and RENEWED. I declared freedom today in Jesus' mighty name. I declare that no past or future mistakes can hold me hostage. I walk boldly in my freedom knowing that you are my great defender, and you will cover me in your love as I embark on the purpose you have for my life. I declare and proclaim that I am FREE.

Amen

Declare It. What invisible chains of the past are you FREE from?

FREEDOM THROUGH FORGIVENESS

How will you be intentional in maintaining your freedom?

Write a personal prayer concerning your freedom.

Yes, my soul, find rest in God; my hope comes from him. Truly he is my rock and my salvation; he is my fortress, I will not be shaken.

Psalm 62:5-6 NIV

Day 12

Rest

The Lord is our firm foundation. Studying His word and communing with Him is what provides us comfort and assurance. God is our peace. We are to rest in Him, and know that there is no battle that He cannot win, no obstacle that He cannot overcome, and no problem that He cannot solve. He is the great I am, we are to seek Him as our refuge, versus fighting the battle in the flesh, and in our own might. Have peace and rest in Him.

Prayer-Prompt

Father God,

Thank you for the privilege to lay my problems, concerns and worries at your feet and rest in you. Teach me how to TRUST solely in you, and rest KNOWING that you are the Great I AM. When I attempt to resort to worry, remind me that you are in control. I acknowledge you as the head of my life. I am aware that you are my provider, protector and healer. Remind me of the wonder of the works that you have already done in my life. Father, I yield to you and desire to rest, trusting in you completely.

Amen

What battles will you lay at His feet today, in exchange for mental and physical rest? Write a personal prayer declaring rest in Him. (Remember to incorporate His word.)

What obstacles or situations will you release control of, in exchange for peace?

You will keep in perfect peace those whose minds are steadfast, because they trust in you.

Isaiah 26:3 NIV

Day 13

Peace

One of God's promises to us is to keep us in perfect peace however; it is up to us to protect the energy that we allow into our personal space. Since The Lord also grants us free will we have the ability to choose who, and what we allow into our lives. We also have free will to make choices regarding our actions, emotions and thought life. Peace is precious, it is more invaluable than words can describe. If you are anything like me, your peace costed you tremendously, and some things have even costed you your peace. Choose your thoughts, actions, emotion, and who you allow into your space wisely. Protect your peace like it cost you something!

Prayer-Prompt

Father God,

Thank you for your perfect peace. Thank you for keeping my heart and mind focused on you. Teach me to remain at peace when the world around me is in a place of uncertainty. Jesus, help me to discern the right company to keep, the right thoughts to think and emotions to feel. Condition me to flow in a positive vibrational frequency so that I may shine the light that you have gifted me, and radiate the energy necessary to attract the right people and circumstances to me. Father, remind me of your promises of love, comfort, and truth, as you keep me in perfect peace.

Amen

How will you intentionally protect your peace mentally, spiritually, emotionally and physically?

Peace of Mind: Do something that makes you feel good. (Journal your experience here)

Write a personal prayer of peace.

I can do all things through him who strengthens me.

Philippians 4:13 ESV

Day 14

Strength

I have to give you all a fair warning. The forgiveness process isn't always an overnight success story. Although the Lord has forgiven us, we have indeed been redeemed trough Christ for our sins, and freed from our past, there will be tests and trials that TRY to come against us. Remember that the Lord, YOUR GOD will strengthen you, and provide you with all that you need to get though. Unforgiving people will not just magically disappear; and while we are working on protecting our peace, there are still going to be people who will "Try" and test you. Regardless of what you are up against, be mindful of the condition of **YOUR** heart, remain prayerful, and remember who your source of strength is! It is no secret; we are often challenged in our weakest most vulnerable areas. Know this, in your weakness is exactly where you will find your strength.

Prayer-Prompt

Father God,

Help me to remember that when I seek you, I shall find my strength. Father God, encourage me to stay in faith, and to put my hope and trust in you, even when I want to give up. Saturate me in your love, and comfort me with your spirit. Remind me that even in the depths of my weakness, and at my lowest point you will be with me. Thank you for being the source of my strength, the light in the darkness, and the peace that surpasses all understanding.

Amen

What area(s) of consistent weakness do you require God's strength in today? Write a personal prayer for strength.

What personal strengths are hindering you from totally submitting to the will of God?

FREEDOM THROUGH FORGIVENESS

*He heals the brokenhearted and binds
up their wounds.*

Psalm 147:3 ESV

Day 15

Trust, and Heal

YOU are WORTH HEALING! BELIEVE that God WILL heal every wound, replace everything that you thought you lost, and give you BEAUTY for ashes! Trust God to HEAL, DELIVER, and RENEW you. TRUST Him to REVIVE your HEART, RECONCILE your marriage and give you PEACE. TRUST Him to give you JOY and STRENGTH. BELIEVE GOD, meditate on His promises and marvel in manifestations of His goodness!

Prayer-Prompt

Father God,

Thank you for healing, delivering, renewing and strengthening ME! I trust you to continue to refine me, and work on me from the inside out, creating a healthier version of me spiritually, mentally, physically, and financially, so that I can become a better reflection of you. Lord when I go astray and lack temperance; remind me of your mercy and forgiveness. Help me to be patient with you as you do a work in me, and to be patient with myself when I don't get things right. I forgive! I am forgiven! I am forgiving in Christ Jesus, and I am ready to walk in my healing and declare peace, restoration, strength and freedom over my life today in Jesus' name.

Amen

How will you trust God? Are there any hidden places that you need God to reveal, and heal?

FREEDOM THROUGH FORGIVENESS

What areas of your life will you surrender and completely trust him to heal?

FREEDOM THROUGH FORGIVENESS

Write a personal freedom through forgiveness declaration. Be detailed and specific. Meditate on it daily

FREEDOM THROUGH FORGIVENESS

Freedom Through Forgiveness Declaration

In the name of Jesus, I declare that I am forgiven, and because I am forgiven, I am FREE.

I forgive myself, and every person who has offended or hurt me.

I hold no grudge or malice in my heart against anyone.

I release everyone from the blame that I have placed upon them.

I am free from the guilt, shame, and condemnation of my past transgressions because God has forgiven me.

I am worthy of God's love.

God loves every ounce of my being; even my imperfections.

God's love poured out on the inside of me is enough.

I declare that His love sustains me.

Because I am loved, I choose to love others the same way that God loves me- unconditionally.

I declare, I am HEALED.

I am DELIVERED.

Every member of my being has been RENEWED in Christ because I have trusted Him to do it.

I have JOY.

I am PEACE.

I have VICTORY.

I declare, that I AM AN OVERCOMER!

In Jesus' name. Amen

Robin "One2Mpower" Major-Oliphant

Scripture Index

Day 1   Forgive

In Him we have redemption through His blood, the forgiveness of sins, in accordance with the riches of God's grace. *Ephesians 1:7 NIV*

Day 2   Love Poured Out

And hope does not put us to shame, because God's love has been poured out into our hearts through the Holy Spirit, who has been given to us. You see, at just the right time, when we were still powerless, Christ died for the ungodly. *Romans 5:5-6*

Day 3   HE's doing a New Thing

Forget the former things; do not dwell on the past. See, I am doing a new thing! Now it springs up; do you not perceive it? I am making a way in the wilderness and streams in the wasteland.   *Isaiah 43:18-19 NIV*

Day 4   Forgive YOU

Therefore, if anyone is in Christ, he is a new creation; old things have passed away; behold, all things have become new. *2 Corinthians 5:17 KJV*

Day 5   The Gift

God saved you by his grace when you believed. And you can't take credit for this; it is a gift from God. *Ephesians 2:8 NLT*

Day 6   Pluck it Away

But the fruit of the Spirit is love, joy, peace, longsuffering, gentleness, goodness, faith, Meekness, temperance: against such there is no law. And they that are Christ's have crucified the flesh with the affections and lusts. If we live in the Spirit, let us also walk in the Spirit. Let us not be desirous of vain glory, provoking one another, envying one another. *Galatians 5:22-26 KJV*

Day 7   Forgive the ALL

Bear with each other and forgive one another if any of you has a grievance against someone. Forgive as the Lord forgave you. *Colossians 3:13 NIV*

Day 8   Quick

Get rid of all bitterness, rage and anger, brawling and slander, along with every form of malice. Be kind and compassionate to one another, forgiving each other, just as in Christ God forgave you. *Ephesians 4:31-32 NIV*

Day 9   Agape

Love is patient, love is kind. It does not envy, it does not boast, it is not proud. It does not dishonor others, it is not self-seeking, it is not easily angered, it keeps no record of wrongs. Love does not delight in evil but rejoices with the truth. It always protects, always trusts, always hopes, always perseveres. *1 Corinthians 13:4-7 NIV*

Day 10   Focus on Him

But seek first his kingdom and his righteousness, and all these things will be given to you as well. *Matthew 6:33 NIV*

Day 11 FREE

 Now the Lord is the Spirit, and where the Spirit of the Lord is, there is freedom. *2 Corinthians 3:17 NIV*

Day 12   Rest

Yes, my soul, find rest in God; my hope comes from him. Truly he is my rock and my salvation; he is my fortress, I will not be shaken. *Psalm 62:5-6 NIV*

Day 13   Peace

You will keep in perfect peace those whose minds are steadfast, because they trust in you. *Isaiah 26:3 NIV*

Day 14   Strength

I   can   do   all   things   through   him   who   strengthens   me. *Philippians 4:13 ESV*

Day 15   Trust, and Heal

He   heals   the   brokenhearted   and   binds   up   their   wounds. *Psalm 147:3 ESV*

OTHER BOOKS FROM THE AUTHOR

From Pieces to Peace: Damaged Goods

From Pieces to Peace: Forgiving the Unforgivable

Freedom Through Forgiveness: An Interactive Prayer Journal and Devotion

Keep in Touch

Connect with me on **Facebook***: One2Mpower*

Follow me on **Instagram***: One2Mpower*

Follow me on **Twitter***: One2Mpower*

Visit my website for booking and event information: www.one2mpower.com

One2Mpower Publishing
One2Mpower@gmail.com

ROBIN MAJOR-OLIPHANT

Made in the USA
Middletown, DE
15 April 2019